Original title:
When I Feel Blue

Copyright © 2024 Creative Arts Management OÜ
All rights reserved.

Author: Lila Davenport
ISBN HARDBACK: 978-9916-88-852-0
ISBN PAPERBACK: 978-9916-88-853-7

A Twilight Tryst with Sadness

In the fading light of day,
Whispers of sorrow play,
Shadows dance on the ground,
In silence, dreams are bound.

The stars begin to glow,
Tears fall soft and slow,
Memories drift like mist,
In the heart, they persist.

A sigh escapes the night,
Lost in the waning light,
Each heartbeat echoes pain,
A bittersweet refrain.

As darkness claims the sky,
Hope begins to sigh,
Yet in the heart's deep chest,
A flicker of rest.

Beneath the Surface of Still Waters

Beneath the surface, secrets lie,
Ripples dance, as whispers sigh.
A tranquil face, the depths conceal,
Nature's heart, a quiet reel.

Light breaks through, a termless play,
Colors blend, then fade away.
What's submerged, yet speaks so loud,
In silent peace, we find the shroud.

A Dance of Dissonance

In clashing tones, the rhythms fight,
A harmony lost beneath the night.
Each twist and turn, a differing stance,
We sway in chaos, the art of chance.

Voices blend, yet drift apart,
A concert born from shattered heart.
In the discord, we find a way,
To dance together, come what may.

The Weight of Unspoken Words

Heavy hangs the word unsaid,
A burdened heart, a weary dread.
In silence echoes what we fear,
Concealed emotions draw us near.

What lingers there, a haunting knife,
Cutting deep into our life.
Still we pause, our thoughts confined,
In trembling breaths, the truth aligned.

Shadows Beneath the Stars

In moonlit nights, the shadows creep,
Secrets hide where silence sleeps.
Beneath the stars, the dreams entwine,
In twilight's grace, our hearts align.

Dancing lights and whispered fears,
Within the dark, we shed our tears.
The universe holds our shared fate,
In cosmic arms, we contemplate.

Hues of a Faded Heart

Once vibrant shades now dim and pale,
Reds of passion begin to fail.
Blues of sorrow, shadows cast,
Colors blend, but hope won't last.

Memories flicker, like distant lights,
Whispers linger on quiet nights.
A canvas stained with joy and pain,
Hues of a heart that loved in vain.

A Wistful Silence Unraveled

In the quiet corners of the mind,
Echoes of dreams we once defined.
Faded whispers in the air,
Moments captured, yet so rare.

Glimmers of laughter, shadows of tears,
Wistfulness lingers through the years.
In silence, stories weave and twine,
A tapestry of love, now benign.

Beneath the Veil of Gloom

Beneath the clouds, a world concealed,
Where hopes and fears remain unsealed.
The sun may rise, but shadows stay,
In a dusk that holds the day at bay.

Rays of light, they struggle to break,
Through the heaviness, the heart would ache.
Yet within gloom, a flicker gleams,
A promise wrapped in quiet dreams.

Echoes of a Melancholy Mind

Thoughts meander through empty halls,
Where silence answers, softly calls.
Each echo carries a weight so deep,
In loneliness, the soul must weep.

Yet in this space, a glimmer grows,
Amidst the sorrow, wisdom flows.
Embracing shadows, light may find,
The beauty held in a melancholy mind.

Echoes in the Abyss

In the depths where shadows dwell,
Whispers weave a haunted spell.
Forgotten dreams like ashes fly,
Echoes linger, fading sigh.

Silent screams in twilight's glow,
Lost in waters deep and slow.
Fragments of a shattered past,
In the abyss, memories cast.

Waves of sorrow rise and fall,
Haunting notes of a distant call.
Through the silence, truths collide,
In the depths, our fears abide.

Yet in darkness, light can bloom,
Hope's soft flame dispels the gloom.
With each echo heard and felt,
A new song of strength is dealt.

Muffled Melancholy

Through gray curtains, sunlight creeps,
In the silence, the heart weeps.
Echoes of a laughter lost,
In the stillness, dreams are tossed.

Shadows dance on walls so bare,
Memories hang like heavy air.
Time drips slowly, like a tear,
Muffled thoughts of what was dear.

A faded picture, worn and torn,
Whispers of a love, forlorn.
In the corners, echoes wait,
Muffled cries that tempt our fate.

Yet in sorrow, beauty hides,
In the depths, resilience bides.
From the quiet, strength will rise,
Muffled hearts will touch the skies.

A Canvas of Grief

Brush strokes thick with shades of blue,
Paint the tales of me and you.
Each hue a tear, each line a sigh,
On this canvas, we learn to cry.

Colors swirl in bittersweet,
Life's canvas bears both love and defeat.
Shadows linger, stories unfold,
In the silence, our truths are told.

With every stroke, a memory flows,
Through the grief, a garden grows.
In the heart of sorrow, we find grace,
A canvas rich in time and space.

From dark to light, the palette shifts,
As healing paints, the spirit lifts.
In the art of loss, we see the way,
A canvas woven in hope's array.

The Weight of Solitude

In the hush of a lonely room,
Echoes linger, shadows loom.
Here in stillness, time feels thick,
The weight of solitude, a heavy pick.

Moments stretch like endless nights,
In quiet corners, lost delights.
Thoughts entwined like fragile threads,
Woven tightly 'round hopes and dreads.

Yet in silence, strength can grow,
In solitude, the heart can know.
The shimmering light of self-discovery,
In the weight, we seek recovery.

For in being alone, we find our way,
To lighter hearts, brighter days.
Through the depths of solitude's mire,
We rise anew, with burning fire.

The Taste of Bitter Rain

Drops fall softly on the ground,
Each one whispers secrets bound.
A flavor sharp, a scent profound,
In every puddle, dreams are drowned.

Gray clouds weep, the sky's embrace,
With every storm, a heart can race.
The taste of sorrow, time can't erase,
In bitter rain, we find our place.

Reflections in a Murky Mirror

In water dark, shadows play,
Fleeting thoughts, they slip away.
Faces twist, truth led astray,
A ghost of self, in disarray.

Waves of doubt coax the unseen,
Who am I in this routine?
Behind the glass, a fading sheen,
Yearning for what might have been.

The Lullaby of Fading Light

As daylight wanes, the stars ignite,
Whispers rise in the soft twilight.
Dreams take flight in the gentle night,
Wrapped in shadows, hearts feel light.

Candles flicker, stories weave,
In every dusk, we choose to believe.
The lullaby of night, we receive,
In fading light, we softly grieve.

Wings of a Withered Butterfly

Frayed edges tell of days gone by,
Once vibrant now, they softly sigh.
A fragile dance, a faint goodbye,
In the garden where dreams lie.

Colors fade, like memories lost,
Every flutter counts the cost.
Though beauty wanes, we are embossed,
In the silence, love is tossed.

Hues of Heartache

A palette of echoes, calls in the night,
Colors of sorrow, shadows take flight.
Whispers of love lost, painted so stark,
Each brushstroke is heavy, etched in the dark.

Memories linger, hues fade away,
Canvas of grief, where dreams used to play.
Splotches of laughter, now flecked with pain,
The heart's aching chambers, forever in vain.

Shadows in My Mind

Lingering whispers, thoughts in the gloom,
Shadows of doubt, in the silence they loom.
  Flickers of light, barely pierce through,
  Chasing the echoes, searching for you.

Every corner turned, brings darkness anew,
 Fragile reflections, of what once was true.
Battles with silence, the heart's heavy bind,
Ghosts of the past, just shadows in my mind.

Emptiness Eclipsed

In the cradle of night, where silence resides,
A void encompasses, where hope often hides.
Stars dimmed by sorrow, a blanket of black,
Emptiness reigns, pulling the light back.

Yet a glimmer appears, on the edge of despair,
A whisper of warmth, floats softly in air.
Hope flickers gently, though shadows persist,
In the heart's quiet chambers, it cannot be missed.

Tears of the Twilight

As daylight surrenders, to evening's embrace,
The world holds its breath, in a delicate space.
Tears rain like droplets, from heavens above,
Twilight collects every whisper of love.

The sky wears a veil, woven from dreams,
Each tear tells a story, or so it seems.
In the stillness of night, all burdens take flight,
Cleansed by the moon's glow, in tears of twilight.

A Heart Adrift

Waves of longing crash so high,
Drifting where the seagulls cry.
In the tempest, dreams collide,
Searching for a place to bide.

Lost in currents, hope feels slight,
Guided only by the night.
Yet within this vast, wide sea,
A heart still beats to be set free.

Dark Clouds on the Horizon

A shadow looms where light once played,
Whispers fill the air, dismayed.
Thunder rumbles, winds take flight,
Chilling hearts, extinguishing light.

Yet beyond the thickened gloom,
Lies a spark, a fragrant bloom.
Hope, though hidden, seeks to rise,
To pierce through darkened, heavy skies.

Solace in the Shadows

In the dim, where silence speaks,
An embrace, a heart that seeks.
Whispers dance through quiet night,
Finding peace in soft twilight.

In shadows deep, a story brews,
Of gentle dreams and hidden hues.
There, in stillness, truths unfold,
A solace found, a heart consoled.

Embracing the Void

In the emptiness, a breath awaits,
A canvas bare, where fate creates.
Silence deep, yet vibrant still,
Curved in shadows, time to fill.

Stepping forth, the unknown sings,
Whispers of potential, open wings.
In the void lies endless space,
With heart alight, I embrace.

Labyrinth of Longing

In a maze where shadows play,
Whispers echo night and day.
Hearts entwined in silent plea,
Searching for what's yet to be.

Winding paths of hope and fear,
Every step draws you near.
Yet the exit fades from sight,
Only shadows hold the light.

In corners where dreams collide,
Yearning souls will often hide.
With each turn, a spark ignites,
Guiding through the endless nights.

At the heart, the truth will gleam,
Love awaits beyond the dream.
In this labyrinth, we find,
The mirror of the heart and mind.

The Sound of Broken Dreams

In the quiet of the night,
Echoes of lost hopes take flight.
Whispers soft like falling rain,
Painting shadows, tinged with pain.

Memories that weave through time,
Play their tune, a haunting chime.
Each note dances in despair,
A melody of silent care.

Fragments of what could have been,
Carefully tucked, held within.
Yet the beauty in the break,
Lies in all the paths we make.

From the ashes, dreams can bloom,
Transcending loss, dispelling gloom.
In the sound, a hope will rise,
A symphony beneath the skies.

Flickers of Dimming Light

In twilight's gentle embrace,
Flickers dance, a slow-paced race.
Moments blend, as shadows sigh,
Whispers fade, yet dreams don't die.

Each spark a tale, a fleeting glance,
Carried forth in twilight's dance.
Stars will blink in soft reply,
Guiding souls as night draws nigh.

In the stillness, shadows creep,
Holding secrets, buried deep.
Yet within the dimming glow,
Hope ignites, refusing woe.

As darkness drapes the weary street,
Find the fire that's bittersweet.
For even in the dimmest night,
Flickers hold the promise bright.

A Solitary Sojourn

On a road less traveled by,
Footsteps echo, soft and shy.
Wanderers seek a distant dream,
In the quiet, spirits stream.

Through the forest, paths unwind,
Nature speaks, the heart aligned.
Mountains rise, a steadfast guide,
In solitude, the soul confides.

Each horizon whispers tales,
Of drifting hopes and gentle gales.
With every turn, a lesson learned,
In the silence, wisdom burned.

So journey forth, embrace the dawn,
In lonely stretches, strength is drawn.
For every step, a story spun,
In solitary sojourn, we're one.

An Umbrella for My Heart

In the storm, I find my peace,
Underneath the shelter here.
Raindrops dance, I watch them fall,
My fears condense, yet I feel clear.

Colors swirl in deepened skies,
My heart, it beats like distant drums.
With every gust, my spirit flies,
An umbrella of hope becomes.

The Silence Shouts

In quiet halls where whispers lay,
The echoes pierce the heavy air.
Words left unspoken lead astray,
Yet in the stillness, hearts lay bare.

Time stretches like a fragile thread,
Between the spaces, pulses thrum.
What isn't said, can still be read,
In silence, countless voices hum.

A Garden of Forgotten Petals

Beneath the weeds, the blossoms fade,
Lost memories cling to the ground.
Once vibrant dreams now softly laid,
In shadows where sweet scents surround.

Yet every petal, bent and torn,
Holds stories inked in hues of time.
From fading blooms, new life is born,
As nature weaves its silent rhyme.

The Void Between Us

A chasm wide, where shadows play,
In every glance, a longing sigh.
Your laughter fades at close of day,
Yet echoes linger, never die.

In that void, I search for light,
Fingertips brushing empty space.
We dance in dreams, beyond the night,
And hope will stitch this heart's embrace.

Shadows of a Sunless Day

In a world where light hides,
Silent whispers linger wide,
Figures dance in muted gray,
Lost in shadows of the day.

Footsteps soft on empty ground,
Where the sun can't be found,
Hope drifts like a fleeting sigh,
Beneath a pale and troubled sky.

Memories wrapped in twilight's thread,
Words unspoken, dreams long fled,
The chill of dusk begins to sway,
In the shadows of a sunless day.

Fading echoes softly play,
In the heart that lost its way,
Yet within the silent fray,
Still there's room for warmth to stay.

Whispers of Forgotten Joy

In the gardens of the past,
Fleeting moments, seldom cast,
Laughter hides in rusted halls,
Amidst the echoing, crumbling walls.

Petals fall from ancient blooms,
Fragrance lost in dusty rooms,
Softly calling from the void,
Whispers speak, though joy's destroyed.

Time weaves tales of what once was,
Shadows dance without a cause,
Faintly flickering, life's bright ploy,
Hums the whispers of forgotten joy.

In the corners where dreams sleep,
Embers buried, secrets keep,
Through the silence, hope's soft ploy,
Glistens still in forgotten joy.

In the Depths of Dull Skies

Clouds roll in, a blanket gray,
Veiling sun, a price to pay,
Every breath feels weighed down low,
In the depths where shadows grow.

A weary heart, a heavy sigh,
Wonders if it's time to fly,
Seeking light amidst despair,
Grasping whispers in the air.

Distant dreams begin to fade,
Echoes of the hope we laid,
Yet in silent, cool twilight,
Stirs the dawn, just out of sight.

Glimmers break the muted scene,
Colors lost, but never mean,
A promise rests within the skies,
In the depths where the soul flies.

The Weight of Unspoken Thoughts

Heavy hearts and silent seams,
Hold the weight of many dreams,
Voices linger, words untold,
In a world that feels so cold.

Thoughts curl tight like autumn leaves,
Trapped in webs that silence weaves,
An unbroken, heavy chain,
Bound to joy, yet steeped in pain.

Eyes that search for what is lost,
Measure love against the cost,
Yet in silence lies a spark,
A flicker in the endless dark.

Still we carry, night and day,
The weight of words we dare not say,
In shadows deep, they twist and reign,
The weight of unspoken thoughts remains.

Unraveled Threads of Hope

In the quiet dusk of dreams,
A whisper stirs the fading light.
Threads of hope begin to gleam,
Amidst the shadows of the night.

Each stitch a promise, softly spun,
A tapestry of love and grace.
From frayed beginnings, we have won,
The strength to find our rightful place.

In every tear, a story weaves,
Of laughter lost and joy regained.
With every heart that truly believes,
The fraying ends are well contained.

So let the colors intertwine,
Each thread a journey, bold and bright.
For in our hearts, the stars align,
Guiding us through the endless night.

The Weight of Unsaid Goodbyes

Silence lingers in the air,
Words unspoken hang like dew.
Burdens carried, hearts laid bare,
A heaviness that feels so true.

Memories dance on the edge of time,
Echoes of laughter, now subdued.
The rhythm of love, lost in rhyme,
As shadows stretch, hearts feel renewed.

Every glance a farewell note,
Each gesture holds a deeper thread.
In the quiet, emotions float,
A testament to words unsaid.

Time moves onward, life prevails,
Yet the weight of the past remains.
In every goodbye, a tale exhales,
Teaching us both joy and pains.

Treading Lightly on Broken Glass

With careful steps, I walk the line,
Fragmented shards beneath my feet.
Each cautious breath, a fleeting sign,
Of strength to find in pain, retreat.

The world reflects in fragile gleam,
A tapestry of sorrow's art.
Yet, in the chaos, hope's a dream,
That leads me bravely through the dark.

Each crunch below tells tales of fear,
But lessons learned forge paths anew.
With every step, I persevere,
The wounds will heal; I shall break through.

So let the moonlight guide my way,
Through jagged paths, I will not stray.
For in the night, I'll find my song,
And rise again, where I belong.

A Symphony of Solitude

In whispers of the dusky night,
A melody begins to play.
Each note a breath, a spark of light,
Resonating in soft array.

The world outside fades to a hum,
As thoughts weave tales of peace and strife.
In solitude, the heart will drum,
Creating rhythms, shaping life.

Harmony in moments spent,
With echoes from the past we share.
An ensemble of intent and lament,
A symphony that fills the air.

In every silence, beauty found,
In solitude, we dance and sway.
For in this quiet, we are bound,
To find ourselves, come what may.

The Quiet Before the Storm

The sky turns gray with a heavy sigh,
Winds whisper secrets, as shadows comply.
Birds take their flight, in a flurry of grace,
Nature holds its breath, in this tranquil space.

Raindrops gather, a soft, gentle tease,
Branches sway softly, in a shivering breeze.
Lightning flickers, a flash in the gloom,
The world waits in stillness, anticipating doom.

Thunder rumbles, a distant drum roll,
The calm before chaos, it grips at the soul.
Hearts race with the thrill of what's yet to come,
In the quiet, the storm's heartbeat begins to hum.

From silence to fury, the earth will transform,
The beauty of nature, in her magical storm.
In the eye of the tempest, we find our own might,
Resilience awakens, in the dark of the night.

Chasing Fleeting Reflections

In mirrors of water, our visions collide,
Ripples of dreams that we once could not hide.
Moments of laughter, like sunlight in trance,
Fade like the echoes of an untold romance.

Footsteps on pathways, where shadows unite,
Fading away with the blush of twilight.
We reach for the colors that dance in our minds,
Yet like fleeting whispers, they drift with the winds.

Chasing the glimmers of time as they flee,
Are we but a shadow of who we should be?
In reflections we linger, as time slips away,
Hoping our dreams do not fade into gray.

Though echoes may vanish, our hopes may take flight,
In the heart of the chase, we find our own light.
A journey worth taking, though moments may lift,
Life's fleeting reflections are the great, cherished gifts.

Beneath a Veil of Silence

Beneath the stillness, secrets softly breathe,
Whispers of the night, woven with the leaves.
Stars flicker gently, in the darkening sky,
Nature's hushed promise, as time drifts by.

The moon casts its glow, a silver-spun thread,
Creating a haven for words left unsaid.
In shadows of dreams, where our spirits entwine,
We find solace sweet, in the quiet divine.

Moments like starlight, precious and rare,
Held in the silence, a bond that we share.
Yet silence can speak, in a language all its own,
A symphony played when we feel most alone.

So in this embrace, let us linger and sway,
For beneath the calm veil, we find our own way.
In the depths of the silence, we learn to believe,
That even in stillness, our hearts can conceive.

Sunsets in Shaded Hues

As daylight retreats, a canvas ignites,
With hues of orange and lavender lights.
The sun bows gracefully, bidding adieu,
Painting horizons in shades bright and true.

Clouds drift like whispers, in cotton-candy skies,
Fleeting moments captured, where beauty lies.
Time slows to savor, in this golden embrace,
Each twilight a treasure, each glance a soft trace.

Reflections in puddles, like dreams set afloat,
Carried on breezes, as shadows devote.
Night blooms around us, as stars start to hum,
In this symphony of colors, an evening's sweet drum.

So let us gather these sunsets so rare,
To weave them in tales, on the strands of our air.
For every hue holds a story, a grace,
In the heart of the sunset, we find our own place.

A Heart Caught in the Rain

Raindrops dance on window panes,
Whispers of love lost in the lanes.
Each droplet a tear from the night,
Filling shadows with fading light.

Clouds gather like thoughts unsaid,
Memories linger where dreams have bled.
A heart left aching in the storm,
Yearning for warmth, a lover's form.

Puddles mirror the skies above,
Reflecting fragments of tender love.
Hope flickers like lightning in dark,
A fleeting promise, a fragile spark.

Yet through the rain, the heart must dare,
To find the beauty hidden there.
For even storms will one day fade,
And open paths to joy remade.

In the Grasp of Sorrow's Hand

In a room where shadows creep,
Sorrow stirs, it whispers deep.
Emptiness clings to weary bones,
Echoes linger in silent tones.

A heart once bright now lost in grey,
Every smile swept far away.
Memories weighed, a heavy shroud,
Loneliness wrapped in a heavy cloud.

Yet in the silence, whispers call,
Reminders of love beyond the fall.
Though darkness grips, a spark may light,
A flicker born from even night.

So in the grasp of sorrow's hand,
Hope must rise, a fragile stand.
For time will heal what pain has wrought,
And joy return, a treasure sought.

Moonlight on a Stained Heart

Moonlight paints the world in silver,
While shadows play, the night does shiver.
A heart once pure now bears the scar,
Of battles fought, both near and far.

Each beam of light a whispered prayer,
For healing found in the night air.
Memories gleam with a bittersweet glow,
As time weaves tales of love and woe.

Stars blink gently in the dark sky,
Holding secrets of days gone by.
They echo softly through the night,
A soft reminder that pain takes flight.

Though stains may linger on the soul,
Love's light can still make the heart whole.
In moonlit moments, dreams revive,
And within shadows, hope may thrive.

Nature's Melancholy Echo

A breeze that whispers through the trees,
Carries with it lost memories.
Leaves fall gently, a quiet sigh,
Nature mourns as seasons die.

Mountains loom with silent grace,
Holding tales time can't erase.
Rivers flow like tears in streams,
Reflecting hopes and faded dreams.

In the dusk, the colors fade,
As twilight wraps the world in shade.
Yet amidst the sorrow, beauty stays,
In every shadow, in every phrase.

Nature's echo sings of pain,
But through the heart, joy may reign.
For in each sigh, a lesson learned,
And from each loss, new fire burned.

A Tranquil Storm

Whispers of wind gently play,
Clouds gather in shades of gray.
Raindrops dance on leaves so green,
Nature's calm, a soothing scene.

Thunder rumbles in the night,
A soft glow of flashes bright.
In the stillness, peace we find,
Heart and soul in sync, aligned.

Lightning paints the skies above,
Reminders of a tempest's love.
Embrace the chaos, let it be,
Within the storm, we feel so free.

As clouds drift away with dawn,
A tranquil world, so fresh, reborn.
The storm has passed, yet echoes stay,
In the calm, we find our way.

Starlit Solitude

Underneath the velvet sky,
Stars awaken, soft and shy.
Whispers carried on the breeze,
Nature's secrets find their ease.

Moonlight bathes the world in grace,
All is quiet in this space.
In the silence, thoughts expand,
Solitude, like grains of sand.

Every twinkle tells a tale,
Journeying where dreams set sail.
In this moment, hearts align,
Starlit solitude, so divine.

As night gives way to morning light,
Here we linger, calm and bright.
In the heavens, souls connect,
In starlit hush, we find respect.

Driftwood Dreams

Along the shore where waters meet,
Driftwood lies in sun's warm seat.
Each piece tells a tale untold,
Carried by tides, brave and bold.

Waves caress the weathered wood,
Memories stirred, a longing good.
In their curves, a wishful sigh,
Dreams take flight beneath the sky.

Barnacles cling, a story spun,
Rustic charm from sea and sun.
Nature's art, a canvas wide,
In driftwood dreams, our thoughts abide.

As the tide draws in so near,
We gather dreams, discard our fear.
On this shore, our hopes ignite,
Driftwood carries them from sight.

The Sound of Silent Cries

In the echoes of the night,
A soft heart seeks the light.
Whispers float on empty air,
Silent cries, a soul laid bare.

Voices trapped within the chest,
Yearning for a moment's rest.
Quiet storms of inner pain,
Silent cries like falling rain.

In a world that often shouts,
Listen close, hear what it doubts.
Every tear holds wisdom deep,
In the silence, secrets keep.

For within the stillness lies,
Every hope and dream that flies.
In the quiet, we may find,
The sound of silent cries, unkind.

Raindrops on a Distant Window

Soft whispers of the rain,
Tracing paths on glass so clear,
Each drop a fleeting thought,
Washing away memories dear.

Clouds embrace the waning day,
Gentle sighs of nature's breath,
In their dance, the shadows play,
A quiet song of fleeting death.

Light fades slowly into night,
Raindrops glide in solemn grace,
Each one carries dreams in flight,
A moment's pause, a silent space.

Windows blur in the soft glow,
Outside worlds look far away,
In this realm, all feelings flow,
Lost in raindrops, I can stay.

Lost in the Mists of Memory

Whispers wrap around my mind,
Faded echoes rise and fall,
Moments held, yet undefined,
In the mists, I hear their call.

Faces drift like autumn leaves,
Carried softly on the breeze,
Each a story that deceives,
Yet brings warmth with gentle ease.

Fragments tangled, hard to find,
Time obscures what once was bright,
Illusions rest in silence bind,
Lost in memory's soft light.

Through the haze, a spark ignites,
Reminding me of love once clear,
In the dark, the heart still fights,
Longing for the days held dear.

The Lingering Gray

In between the night and dawn,
A shroud of gray begins to rise,
Whispers of a day withdrawn,
Painting clouds across the skies.

The sun seems lost in shadow's grasp,
Hesitant in its glowing light,
Hope holds tightly, yet must clasp,
The dream of day to chase the night.

Each step feels uncertain, slow,
As if the world holds its breath,
In this silence, time does flow,
A dance of life, a waltz with death.

Yet in the gray, we find a pause,
Moments wrapped in tranquil grace,
Welcoming what the heart finds cause,
Embracing change, we find our place.

Morning Without Light

A dawn that holds no sunlit cheer,
Wrapped in shadows, cold and bare,
Each breath a whisper steeped in fear,
A world awash in muted air.

Chill of night still clings to skin,
Dreams retreat into the haze,
The heart seeks warmth that's drawn within,
Waiting for the day to blaze.

Hope flickers like a candle low,
Fighting back the tendrils gray,
Longing for the light to grow,
To break the weight of dismal play.

Yet in this silence, strength we find,
Tomorrow's promise holds its spark,
In morning's dark, we are aligned,
Together shining in the stark.

Clouds of Comfort Reversed

Soft whispers float in the air,
Gentle breezes, light as care.
Yet hidden storms begin to rise,
Veiling sunshine, masking skies.

The warmth once felt has slipped away,
Clouds gather, turning bright to gray.
What once was peace now brings a sigh,
A dance of shadows passing by.

In the twilight, dreams take flight,
Seeking solace, lost from sight.
Drifting softly, lost in thought,
Searching for the love once sought.

But within the storm, a spark remains,
Hope flickers, through the pains.
Clouds may shadow, yet they show,
That comfort lies in letting go.

The Lingering Kiss of Loneliness

In silent rooms where echoes dwell,
A whisper holds a secret spell.
Loneliness wraps like a shroud,
In empty spaces, lost and proud.

Familiar faces fade from sight,
Shadows stretch in dim twilight.
A lingering kiss, soft yet stark,
Leaves a mark, a tender scar.

The heart beats on in muted tones,
Yearning for warmth, a touch of bones.
Yet in the quiet, strength can grow,
Finding light in undertow.

With every sigh, a new chance blooms,
To dance among the silent rooms.
From sadness springs a sturdy seed,
A path of hope takes lonely lead.

Threads of an Unraveled Dream

Waking hours blend into night,
Fragments dance, just out of sight.
Threads pulled loose from a tapestry,
Whispers of what is yet to be.

In visions lost, the heart does roam,
Seeking solace, finding home.
Each twist and turn a tale to weave,
In the quiet, we learn to believe.

The colors fade but memories last,
Echoes of joys, shadows cast.
Unraveled dreams call for repair,
Sewing pieces with loving care.

With every stitch, we redefine,
Creating paths that intertwine.
Through mending hearts, new dreams will flow,
Threads of a past create tomorrow.

Moments Lost in Blue Shadows

In every hour, traces remain,
Fragments of joy, whispers of pain.
Moments lost in twilight's grace,
Captured glances, a fleeting embrace.

Blue shadows cast on forgotten dreams,
Silhouette dances, or so it seems.
A tender wish carried on air,
Glimmers of hope, scattered with care.

Time slips softly, like grains of sand,
Each moment fleeting, yet so grand.
Count the stars that dared to shine,
In shades of blue, their light divine.

Though shadows linger in the night,
Memories glow with a gentle light.
For in the depths, we find our way,
Moments cherished, not gone astray.

An Ocean of Quietude

Waves whisper secrets to the shore,
A stillness lingers, forevermore.
The sun dips low, painting the sea,
In peaceful hues, it calls to me.

Gentle tides pull at my soul's core,
Each ebb and flow, I long to explore.
The horizon stretches, vast and wide,
In this quietude, my dreams abide.

Seagulls glide in the dusky air,
Their cries are soft, a tender prayer.
With every breath, I find my peace,
As the world's worries slowly cease.

In this calm embrace, I find my home,
An ocean of stillness where I roam.
The heartbeats sync with nature's song,
In the ocean of quietude, I belong.

The Color of Dusk

Golden hues blend with shades of grey,
As daylight slowly fades away.
Clouds blush softly, a tender kiss,
In the quiet, I find my bliss.

Whispers of night call in the light,
Painting the sky with stars so bright.
Each breath is filled with fleeting time,
Dusk dances softly, a silent rhyme.

The horizon glows like embers' breath,
A canvas alive, embracing death.
Yet in this moment, life holds sway,
The color of dusk, a bright bouquet.

I linger here, beneath the sky,
As dreams take flight and moments fly.
In every shadow, a story unfolds,
In the color of dusk, life still upholds.

The Tomorrow That Could Have Been

Winds of tomorrow whisper low,
Tales of paths we'll never know.
Footsteps echo in empty halls,
The dreams we lost, the silent calls.

Time's river flows with hidden strands,
Choices made with trembling hands.
What ifs linger in shadowed light,
A tapestry woven in endless night.

Faces fade in memories' haze,
The tomorrow lost in yesterday's maze.
Hope clings tight, yet drifts away,
In the quiet, our hearts still sway.

Yet in the dark, a spark may gleam,
Futures lived in the depth of dream.
For every end, a new beginning waits,
The tomorrow that could have been, still relates.

Veiled Horizons

A misty veil hangs over the hills,
Softly it shrouds the world in chills.
Secrets linger in the morning dew,
Veiled horizons, unknown and new.

Mountains loom with grandeur untold,
Whispers of stories in silence unfold.
Each step a journey, each breath a chance,
Veiled horizons invite the dance.

The beauty lies in what we can't see,
In hidden wonders, we long to be free.
A heart's exploration, a soul's desire,
Each horizon leads to new fire.

Beneath the veil, the world awaits,
With open arms and welcoming gates.
In each new dawn, we boldly stride,
To veiled horizons, where dreams abide.

Pages Torn from Yesterday

Faded ink upon the page,
Whispers of forgotten dreams,
Time has worn the fragile edge,
Lost in soft, silent screams.

Memories like autumn leaves,
Drifting on a restless breeze,
Moments trapped in tattered scripts,
Buried deep, never to cease.

Each turn brings a muted sigh,
Stories left to quietly fade,
Pages torn, but hearts still try,
To mend the scars that they made.

In the book of days gone by,
Lessons learned, some smiles lost,
Holding on as we say goodbye,
Embracing all that was the cost.

Glass Shards of Longing

Reflections dance on fractured light,
Fragments of a time once bright,
Shattered hopes in silver hue,
Echoes of what we once knew.

Each shard a story left untold,
Wishes etched in shades of gold,
Piecing dreams with tender care,
In the silence, we lay bare.

Fingers trace the broken lines,
Searching through the tangled signs,
In our hearts, the longing stays,
Filling up the empty days.

Yet through the pain, we find delight,
Building castles from the night,
In the shards, a beauty gleams,
As we chase our fractured dreams.

The Echo of Lonely Nights

Moonlight casts a silver glow,
Whispers linger, soft and low,
In the stillness, shadows speak,
Truths are found where hearts are weak.

Each tick of time a gentle sigh,
Lonely thoughts that drift and fly,
Haunting melodies of the past,
Fleeting moments, shadows cast.

Stars above in silent gaze,
Watch the world through dusky haze,
In the dark, we find our fate,
Echoes of love that still await.

Tomorrow holds a faint promise,
Yet the night knows all our dreams,
In the quiet, softly hums,
The echo of what each heart means.

Weight of Wistfulness

Heavy hangs the air of thought,
Carrying dreams that time forgot,
Burdens wrapped in soft regret,
Lost chances we can't forget.

Gentle sighs and fleeting glances,
In the heart, a dance of chances,
Memories like feathers fall,
Graceful moments, bittersweet call.

Yearning hearts in shadows dwell,
Searching for that magic spell,
In the stillness, hope ignites,
Chasing down the quiet nights.

Yet through it all, a flame remains,
Whispering through joy and pains,
In wistfulness, we find a way,
To treasure every heartbeat's sway.

Remnants of Radiance

Fleeting light in twilight's embrace,
Whispers of warmth in a shadow's place.
Echoes of laughter, soft and clear,
Memories linger, forever near.

In the garden where flowers bloom,
Colors fade, yet chase away gloom.
Each petal holds a story untold,
Glimmers of hope in hues of gold.

Through the dusk, the stars ignite,
Guiding the lost with gentle light.
Time may pass, yet still remains,
Remnants of joy amidst the pains.

In the stillness of night's caress,
Radiance flickers, a soft finesse.
Holding tight to what once shone bright,
Preserving the warmth in the cool night.

The Last Laugh of Lavender

In fields of purple, silence sings,
A gentle breeze, the joy it brings.
Lavender sways, a soft ballet,
Whispers of laughter dance away.

As sun dips low, shadows grow long,
Each petal's breath, a soothing song.
Flecks of dusk weave through the haze,
A final bow, the lavender sways.

With the twilight, secrets unfold,
Stories of love in hues so bold.
The day departs, yet smiles remain,
In lavender's heart, joy will reign.

A fleeting glance, the night draws near,
Softly it echoes, laughter clear.
In dreams we'll wander, hand in hand,
Through fields of lavender, forever stand.

Songs of a Silent Storm

Whispers collide in a shadowed realm,
The hush of thunder, nature's helm.
Raindrops tap like soft-spun dreams,
While silence breaks at the edge of screams.

Clouds embrace like lovers torn,
Each droplet sings, a life reborn.
Caught in the dance of twilight's grace,
The storm unfolds, a wild embrace.

In the eye where calmness lies,
Soft notes echo, beneath stormy skies.
A symphony brewed in thunder's hand,
Resounding strength across the land.

With each heartbeat, nature's song,
The silent storm won't linger long.
Yet love persists in echoes deep,
As the tempest wakes from its sleep.

Glistening Tears on a Willow

Beneath the boughs of a sorrowed tree,
Glistening tears, set the heart free.
Willow's embrace, a tender guide,
Where shadows linger, and dreams reside.

In the silence, stories weave,
Whispers of loss, yet learn to believe.
Each droplet shines in the morning light,
Carrying burdens, transforming fright.

Branches sway to a sorrowed tune,
Dancing softly, beneath the moon.
Every tear reflects the past,
A glimpse of pain that won't hold fast.

In the gentleness of twilight's breath,
Tears turn to memories, life after death.
With open arms, the willow stands,
Glistening tears held in tender hands.

Chasing Echoes of Forgotten Laughter

In the hollow of the night, we roam,
Whispers of joy in a twilight dome.
Echoes linger where shadows play,
Fleeting moments drift away.

Faces fade in the rearview glass,
Memories caught like blades of grass.
We laugh to fill the empty spaces,
Chasing echoes of forgotten praises.

A song once sweet, now barely heard,
Fading softly like a passing bird.
Yet in the silence, a spark ignites,
Reviving dreams in the moonlit nights.

Among the stars, we search for light,
Recovering laughter from the night.
In the dance of shadows, we entwine,
Reviving echoes where love may shine.

The Longing for a Brighter Dawn

In the stillness before the rise,
Hope awaits 'neath painted skies.
A whisper stirs the heavy air,
Longing hearts are left bare.

Each moment drags like fading night,
A flicker yearns for morning light.
Promises dance in the twilight haze,
A brighter dawn holds its gaze.

With every breath, we wait in sighs,
For sunlit paths where solace lies.
Fears released to the gentle breeze,
Awakening strength among the trees.

As shadows fade, the day unwinds,
Hope intertwines with open minds.
We rise again on wings of trust,
A brighter dawn, our hearts adjust.

Beneath the Weight of Expectation

Carrying dreams upon our backs,
We tread the path through thickest tracks.
Each step a burden, heavy and bold,
Beneath the weight of stories untold.

Eyes are cast toward distant peaks,
In silent moments, the heart speaks.
With every pulse, we forge ahead,
Chasing hopes that fill us with dread.

Yet within this strain, we find our spark,
A fire ignites from the deepest dark.
Resilience blooms like flowers in spring,
Beneath the weight, our spirits sing.

So let us rise, with strength reborn,
Unraveling threads where dreams are worn.
The world awaits our eager hands,
To carve our path on shifting sands.

Autumn Leaves Like Broken Promises

Golden whispers drift from trees,
Promises scattered like autumn leaves.
Each one a memory softly lies,
Fading dreams beneath gray skies.

Crisp air carries tales of change,
A chapter turned, a life strange.
In the rustling, we hear the plea,
Of what we were, what's yet to be.

As colors fade, we gather near,
To mourn the dreams we hold so dear.
Yet in the silence, wisdom gleams,
From broken promises, new dreams teem.

So let us dance among the falls,
Embracing warmth as winter calls.
For every leaf that drifts away,
A brighter truth finds its way.

The Dance of Hidden Tears

In shadows deep, emotions sway,
Whispers brush the heart's ballet.
Each drop that falls, a silent song,
A hidden dance where souls belong.

Beneath the mask, a quiet storm,
A fragile heart, yet feels so warm.
With every sigh, a story weaves,
In tears of joy, the spirit grieves.

The moonlight casts a gentle gleam,
On memories lost, and hopes that beam.
Through veils of grief, we learn to see,
The beauty wrapped in mystery.

So let them flow, those hidden tears,
For in their dance, we face our fears.
In sorrow's waltz, we find our grace,
A healing pulse in time and space.

A Garden of Dying Petals

Amidst the blooms, the colors fade,
Once vibrant hues now softly laid.
Each petal drops, a whispered sigh,
In nature's hand, the time to die.

Yet beauty lingers in decay,
In withered grace, the night meets day.
The cycle spins, though hearts may ache,
From dying blooms, new life will wake.

The fragrance lingers, a sweet farewell,
As memories weave their timeless spell.
In the garden's arms, we let them go,
For every end, a seed to sow.

So cherish now, the fleeting phase,
In dying petals, life's soft praise.
For every end that we might mourn,
Is but the place where hope is born.

Solitude in a Crowded Room

Voices echo, laughter swirls,
Yet in my heart, a stillness unfurls.
Faces pass like fleeting dreams,
In crowded thoughts, I drift, it seems.

The air is thick with shared delight,
But in my core, I seek the light.
A gentle whisper, a silent plea,
In solitude, I long to be free.

Connections fade, like shadows cast,
In this great hall, I feel outcast.
Desire for depth in shallow streams,
In crowded spaces, lost in dreams.

But solace waits in quiet nooks,
Where silence breathes in hidden books.
In solitude, my spirit finds,
The clarity the world unwinds.

Beneath the Surface of a Stilled Lake

A mirror calm, reflecting skies,
Beneath the stillness, secret lies.
In depths unseen, the currents flow,
Where shadows dance, and silence grows.

The lilies float, like thoughts untold,
In tranquil hues of green and gold.
Yet under peace, the pulses race,
In gentle tides, we find our place.

Ripples soft, as breezes play,
With every wave, the world gives way.
In the depths, the stories twist,
Of hidden dreams we dare not list.

So dive within, where waters gleam,
To seek the truth behind the dream.
For in the depths, we find our fate,
Beneath the calm of the stilled lake.

Dreams Wrapped in Gray

In the morning mist, they fade,
Whispers of wishes, softly laid.
Clouded thoughts drift through the air,
Chasing phantoms, unaware.

Shadows dance on faded walls,
Echoing laughter, distant calls.
In twilight's grasp, dreams intertwine,
Colors dulled, yet still divine.

Each sigh conceals a secret ache,
Lost in the silence that we make.
Frayed edges of what once was bright,
Embrace the gray, await the light.

But in that haze, hope still gleams,
In the quiet, we find our dreams.
Wrapped in gray, yet still we soar,
Through the shroud, we yearn for more.

The Burden of a Heavy Heart

Beneath the weight of silent tears,
Lies a tale of tangled fears.
A heart encased in sorrow's hold,
Stories of love, left untold.

Each beat a whisper of despair,
Echoes linger in the air.
Longing for the light to break,
Heavy burdens, hard to shake.

In shadows deep, the memories dwell,
Of fleeting joy, and timeless hell.
Yet in the gloom, a flicker stays,
A spark of hope, in darkest days.

Through heavy fog, we seek the dawn,
In the fight to carry on.
Though burdens weigh, we find the way,
To lift our hearts, and seize the day.

A Symphony of Stillness

In the hush of twilight's glow,
Nature sings a soft, slow flow.
The world pauses, breath held tight,
In silence found, there lies the light.

Leaves whisper secrets to the breeze,
Time stands still, with such sweet ease.
Beneath the stars, our hearts align,
In this moment, pure, divine.

Raindrops kiss the thirsty ground,
In every droplet, peace is found.
Listen close, the evening calls,
A symphony where silence falls.

Every heartbeat finds its tune,
The moon hums softly, cradling soon.
In stillness, we become the song,
Together, where we all belong.

Floating on a Sea of Sorrow

Drifting slowly on the tide,
A heart adrift, nowhere to hide.
Waves of gray crash on the shore,
Each whisper pulls me from the core.

Glimmers of joy, so hard to find,
Lost in the depths of a restless mind.
Memories weave through the ocean's swell,
In this silence, I know too well.

Yet in the deep, a spark remains,
A flicker of hope among the strains.
Floating softly, still I dream,
In the sorrow, I learn to scheme.

With each wave, a lesson learned,
In the tempest, my spirit burned.
Finding strength in sorrow's flow,
Floating free, through depths I go.

The Heartbeat of Absent Smiles

In shadows cast by fading light,
Where laughter once danced through the night.
Echoes linger in empty air,
A silent prayer for those who care.

Memories flicker like fragile flames,
Fragments of joy entwined with names.
The heartbeat of absent smiles can be,
A haunting reminder of what used to be.

In every corner, a sigh remains,
Whispers of love, now bound by chains.
Yet hope flickers in the quiet dark,
A promise held in a single spark.

Still, the world spins in gentle grace,
Time unwinds in a slow embrace.
With each step through the haunting past,
We find the strength to love at last.

In the Quiet of a Sleepy Village.

In the quiet of a sleepy town,
Where rooftops wear a golden crown.
Time moves slowly, as shadows play,
A lullaby to end the day.

Children's laughter weaves through streets,
As evening whispers softly greets.
The scent of flowers fills the air,
In this haven, free from care.

Windows glow with warm, soft light,
Each family cherished, holding tight.
Stories linger like fragrant tea,
Binding hearts in harmony.

Beneath the stars, old tales unfold,
Of dreams and hopes, both brave and bold.
In this village, hearts align,
In the quiet, life feels divine.

Shades of Sorrow

In twilight's grip, the shadows creep,
Where memories linger, silent weep.
The colors fade, a world turned gray,
In the shades of sorrow, dreams decay.

A wilting flower, the petals fall,
Echoing whispers from the past's call.
Each breath a burden, heavy and true,
Carrying tales the heart once knew.

Yet in this darkness, a spark may glow,
A glimmer of hope, amidst the woe.
In shades of sorrow, life finds a way,
To blossom anew at the break of day.

So let the tears wash away the fear,
For every loss brings something dear.
In the palette of pain, love draws near,
Painting a portrait, forever clear.

Whispers of Gloom

In the corners where shadows loom,
Echoes linger, whispers of gloom.
The night drapes softly, a heavy veil,
Where dreams once soared now seem frail.

Lonesome winds carry tales untold,
Of hearts once vibrant, now grown cold.
In the silence, a heavy sigh,
In the whispers of gloom, hope seems shy.

Yet deep in the darkness, a flicker remains,
A sliver of light that still sustains.
In every sorrow, a lesson to learn,
In whispers of gloom, the soul will yearn.

So let the shadows dance their dance,
For in their grip, we find our chance.
To rise anew from the depths below,
In the whispers of gloom, love will flow.

Cracks in the Smiling Facade

Behind the laughter, shadows creep,
An unseen weight, secrets to keep.
With every smile, a silent plea,
A fragile heart, longing to be free.

In crowded rooms, a lonely face,
Worn out shoes in a weary race.
The mask slips down, just for a while,
Revealing cracks in the painted smile.

A Wistful Pause

Beneath the stars, I stop and think,
Memories swirl in twilight's ink.
A moment held in night's gentle glow,
Yearning for what I used to know.

Time holds stories that we once shared,
Yet in the silence, I'm unprepared.
A wistful pause, a fleeting glance,
Lost in the echoes of a forgotten dance.

Fragments of Forgotten Joy

Scattered pieces of laughter bright,
Now only whispers in fading light.
A photograph, worn edges fray,
Capturing moments that slipped away.

Year by year, the colors fade,
Yet in the heart, the fragments stayed.
Embers of joy in the softest glow,
Reminding us of the love we know.

Floating in Deep Waters

In deep waters where shadows lie,
I drift along, with dreams to fly.
Each ripple sings of tales untold,
Beneath the surface, treasures of gold.

I feel the pull of the ocean's call,
Weightless, I dance through the rise and fall.
Floating free where the currents blend,
In the depths I find my journey's end.

Driftwood Memories

On the shore where dreams lay bare,
Forgotten whispers fill the air.
Waves collide, erasing pain,
Nature's art, a timeless gain.

Fragments of laughter, tides they chase,
Carved by time in a gentle embrace.
Salt and sun, they tell their tale,
Of love once lost, a fleeting sail.

Starlit nights under a moonlit sky,
Echoes of joy as the seagulls cry.
Driftwood memories, soft and sweet,
A dance of life, where hearts once meet.

Each piece a story, each turn a chance,
In nature's rhythm, we find our dance.
With every tide, our spirits roam,
In driftwood memories, we find our home.

The Portrait of Regret

In shadows cast by a fading light,
A portrait hangs, a haunting sight.
Brushstrokes murmur of paths not taken,
An artist's vision, forever shaken.

Colors bleed into the night,
Each hue a tale of lost delight.
Eyes that stare, yet cannot see,
The mirror reflects who we should be.

Time erodes what once was bright,
A canvas marred by quiet fright.
Forgotten dreams in frames confined,
Life's masterpiece, unrefined.

Yet within the lines, some hope remains,
To learn from sorrow, to break the chains.
In every smudge, a chance to mend,
The portrait of regret—a path to transcend.

Fading Footprints in the Sand

Along the shore, where tides retreat,
Footprints linger, a dance so sweet.
Waves wash over, erasing time,
Memories drift, like an old rhyme.

Each step a story, each path a chance,
In the golden glow, we find romance.
Sunrise glimmers on grains of gold,
Moments cherished, yet never told.

Yet the ocean's call is loud and strong,
Pulling our hearts, where we belong.
Fading footprints, where we stand,
A fleeting mark on shifting sand.

As tides renew, we learn to cope,
In every wave, we find our hope.
Fading footprints, a dance of grace,
Life's journey, an endless race.

Serenity in the Shadows

In twilight's hush, the shadows fall,
Whispers of peace, a calming call.
Beneath the boughs, where silence reigns,
Nature's breath, where stillness gains.

Softly the stars begin to gleam,
Casting their light on a forgotten dream.
In every rustle, a gentle sigh,
Serenity whispers, as time drifts by.

Moonbeams dance on the forest floor,
Opening paths to a hidden door.
In the embrace of the night so deep,
Nature cradles all that we keep.

In shadows, life finds its way,
Wisdom grows in the shades of gray.
Serenity blooms in the quiet space,
A sanctuary, our sacred place.

Milton Keynes UK
Ingram Content Group UK Ltd.
UKHW020151291024
450401UK00007B/111